BETTER BUSINESS WRITING

REVISED EDITION

Susan L. Brock

CRISP PUBLICATIONS, INC.
Los Altos, California

BETTER BUSINESS WRITING
REVISED EDITION

I would like to acknowledge the following individuals for their excellent help reviewing earlier drafts of this manuscript. The comments and suggestions were valuable in preparing the final manuscript.

My sincere thanks to:
Patricia P. Harper—Supervisor, Secretarial Training, Amoco Corporation
Ray Shepard—Professor, English Department, Hinds Junior College, Mississippi
Bernadine P. Branchaw—Professor, College of Business, Western Michigan University
Jack Swenson—Instructor, Canãda College, California.

                              Susan L. Brock

CREDITS
Editor: **Michael G. Crisp**
Designer: **Carol Harris**
Typesetting: **Interface Studio**
Cover Design: **Carol Harris**
Artwork: **Ralph Mapson**

Crisp books are distributed in Canada by Reid Publishing, Ltd., P.O. Box 7267, Oakville, Ontario, Canada L6J 6L6.

In Australia by Career Builders, P.O. Box 1051 Springwood, Brisbane, Queensland, Australia 4127.

And in New Zealand by Career Builders, P.O. Box 571, Manurewa, New Zealand.

Library of Congress Catalog Card Number 86-72079
Brock, Susan L.
Better Business Writing
ISBN 0-931961-25-4

PREFACE

American businesses reportedly lose $1 billion a year due to "foggy" writing that wastes time, kills contracts, and alienates customers. You don't have to be part of this problem. This book is designed to teach you the basics you need to become a more effective writer. The accompanying exercises will enhance your writing skills and are relevant to the practical demands of the business world.

By the time you complete this brief book, you will be better prepared to write a clear, concise business letter, memo, and report. The best way to improve your writing is to write often. You'll find if you routinely practice the techniques in this book, your writing skills will continue to improve. When this happens, you're on your way to writing more clearly, concisely, and humanely, and this will make you more effective at work.

A voluntary learning contract is available on page 69. It is a good starting point if you are serious about getting the most from this book. Good luck and don't give up! Writing well is hard work, but your career is worth it.

Susan L. Brock

Susan L. Brock

ABOUT THIS BOOK

BETTER BUSINESS WRITING is not like most books. It has a unique "self-paced" format that encourages a reader to become personally involved. Designed to be "read with a pencil," there are an abundance of exercises and activities that invite participation.

The objective of BETTER BUSINESS WRITING is to help people improve the quality of their writing skills by providing some basic concepts and allowing the readers to practice what they have learned.

BETTER BUSINESS WRITING (and the other self-improvement books listed at the back of the book) is valuable in several ways. Here are some possibilities:

—**Individual Study.** Because the book is self-instructional, all that is needed is a quiet place, some time and a pencil. Completing the activities and exercises, will provide practical steps for self-improvement.

—**Workshops and Seminars.** This book is ideal as pre-assigned reading prior to a formal training session. With the basics in hand, more time can be spent on concept extensions and advanced applications. The book is also effective when used as part of a workshop or seminar.

—**Remote Location Training.** Copies can be sent to those not able to attend "home office" training sessions. BETTER BUSINESS WRITING also makes an excellent "desk reference book."

There are other possibilities that depend on the needs or objectives of the user. You are invited to find uses that will provide benefits for your program.

CONTENTS

INTRODUCTION:
Self-Assessment   3
Personality Types   4
PART 1: BACK TO BASICS—SPELLING, PUNCTUATION & USAGE
Spelling Exercise   7
Spelling Mnemonics   8
Punctuation Pointers   11
Punctuation Exercise   13
A Usage Quiz   16
PART 2: STYLE
Wordiness Exercise I   19
(Unnecessary) Redundancies   21
Wordiness Exercise II   22
Pitfalls of Business Writing   23
Five Stylistic Tools   29
PART 3: BUSINESS WRITING
Business Writing—Practical Samples   30
  Business Letter   31
  Employment Agency Counselor's Letter   33
  Business Memo   35
  Nine Tips for a Better Memo   36
  Conveying Bad News Tactfully   37
  Sample ''Bad News'' Memo   38
Basic Outline for Business Letters   40
Sample Outlined Letter   43
Avoiding Sexism in Business Writing   45
Writing Business Letters—Exercise   46
PART 4: WRITING PERSUASIVELY
Persuasion—Bits and Pieces   49
The Motivated Sequence Outline   51
A Model of the Motivated Sequence Outline   52
Writing Persuasively—An Exercise   55
REVIEW
The Ten Commandments for More Effective Communication   57
APPENDIX: SOLUTIONS AND AUTHOR RESPONSE TO EXERCISES
Voluntary Learning Contract   69

HOW WELL DO YOU KNOW YOUR WRITING ABILITIES?

Before you begin, take a minute to assess your writing style. You may discover you know a lot more than you think, or you may discover specific areas where you need to improve. Either way the exercise on the facing page will help you assess your writing ability. Read each statement, and mark the response that applies to you.

SELF-ASSESSMENT

	YES	NO	I DON'T KNOW
1. I always keep my audience in mind when I write.	☐	☐	☐
2. I have no problem with the basics: grammar, spelling, and punctuation.	☐	☐	☐
3. I know the difference between active and passive construction.	☐	☐	☐
4. I choose simple words to communicate clearly.	☐	☐	☐
5. I make it a point to state clearly the specific purpose of my letters or memos.	☐	☐	☐
6. I recognize and avoid business clichés and jargon.	☐	☐	☐
7. I ruthlessly edit everything I write.	☐	☐	☐
8. I'm confident I can communicate persuasively.	☐	☐	☐

Don't worry if you weren't sure of the significance of any of the above questions. As you proceed through this book, each will be clearly explained. Soon, you'll be able to mark each statement in this self-assessment with a YES!

4

PERSONALITY TYPES

Before you begin to write anything, consider your audience. If you have some insight into the personality of your reader, you'll have an opportunity to tailor your writing to make it compatible with that personality. For example, if your reader is logical and analytical, your letter must be thorough and detailed. What could be more flattering to a reader than to receive a letter or memo written specifically with him or her in mind? The addition of a ''human element'' is so often missing in the business world.

Following are descriptions of four personality types which are based on psychologist Carl Jung's theory.

I. THINKERS

1. Description: analytical, logical, self-controlled, stubborn, detail-oriented, aloof, critical, skeptical, conservative, noncommital.
2. Strengths: perfectionist, well organized, objective, rational, conceptual, persistent, accurate, orderly, hard working.
3. Weaknesses: indecisive, insensitive, inflexible, slow, judgmental.
4. Common jobs: accountant, banker, attorney, doctor, scientist, clerk, engineer, computer programer, teacher.
5. Opposite style: Feeler

II. SENSORS

1. Description: action-oriented, results-oriented, task-oriented, workaholic, confident, hard-charging, determined, tough, competitive.
2. Strengths: pragmatic, assertive, directional, competitive, confident, disciplined in using time, receptive to options.
3. Weaknesses: domineering, arrogant, status-seeking, emotionally cold, impulsive, autocratic, inattentive, impersonal.
4. Common jobs: athlete, manager, executive, coach, truck driver, entrepreneur, pilot, doctor.
5. Opposite style: Intuitor

OBSERVATIONS: These two types are common in the business world. They have different approaches to understanding and appreciating letters. Above all, the *Thinker Type* wants thoroughness and detail; the *Sensor Type* wants to know the ''bottom line.'' Consider the personality type of your reader in everything you write.

PERSONALITY TYPES (continued)

III. FEELERS

1. Description: emotional, caring, introspective, melancholic, sympathetic, diplomatic, persuasive, entertaining, warm, friendly, agreeable, dependable, stable.

2. Strengths: spontaneous, persuasive, empathic, probing, loyal, warm, supportive, dependable, sensitive.

3. Weaknesses: impulsive, sentimental, procrastinating, subjective, oversensitive, overly cautious.

4. Common jobs: nurse, secretary, teacher, social worker, salesperson, psychiatrist.

5. Opposite style: Thinker

IV. INTUITORS

1. Description: creative, reflective, quiet, scholarly, reserved, conceptual, intelligent, enthusiastic, personable, gregarious, impatient, involved, assertive.

2. Strengths: original, conceptual, warm and approachable, stimulating, adventurous, sensitive, receptive to new ideas, creative, idealistic, flexible.

3. Weaknesses: unrealistic, devious, impractical, manipulative, undisciplined in use of time, uncontrolled.

4. Common jobs: scientist, researcher, artist, professor, writer, corporate planner, advertising person.

5. Opposite style: Sensor

OBSERVATIONS: *Feeler* and *Intuitor* types are less common in the business world. If your reader possesses these traits, your letters to him or her need to be human. Because so much business writing seems mechanical and computer-generated, the *Feeler* and *Intuitor* will appreciate it if you remember that writing is a personal transaction between people.

PART 1   BACK TO BASICS— SPELLING, PUNCTUATION AND USAGE

You may be approaching this section with discomfort. Despite your fears, you will find it is relatively painless—in part because it's short, and also because it concentrates only on the most common errors people typically make. The basics include spelling, punctuation, and usage. We'll briefly review each.

Many people acquire bad habits in mechanics and usage before leaving school. The purpose of this section is to strengthen your skills in the basics. If this section does nothing more than correct a single error you repeatedly make, your writing will improve because of it.

The exercise on the facing page tests your spelling skills. Please read each sentence and complete the blanks with the correctly spelled word suggested in the parentheses. After you complete the exercise, turn to page 60 to check your answers. Don't worry if you miss a few; the sentences contain commonly misspelled words. Review this section again once you have completed this book to ensure you have learned to correctly spell each item.

THIS WAY TO BETTER SPELLING

SPELLING EXERCISE

DIRECTIONS: Fill in the missing letters to spell the word correctly. Check your answers with those on page 60.

1. The applicant studied Freudian _____ (-chology) in college.

2. Ms. Brown wanted us to sit _____ (tog-th-r) at the meeting so we would not be _____ (sep-r-ted) when the meeting was over.

3. The new hotel can _____ (acco-date) up to 1,500 guests.

4. This memo _____ (super-edes) the _____ (prec-ding) one, which was distributed last week.

5. The Hospital _____ (Ben-fit) raised a lot of money for the children's wing.

6. It never _____ (oc-ur-ed) to us that the _____ (gove-ment) might increase our taxes.

7. The secretary's boss _____ (of-er-ed) her a bonus if she would _____ (proc-d) to enroll in a shorthand class.

8. We successfully avoided an _____ (arg-ment) when we discussed changing the _____ (envi-ment) of the office to boost employee morale.

9. The hinges on the door are _____ (l-se), and it _____ (consist-ntly) rattles when opened.

10. It would be difficult not to _____ (bel-ve) the results.

TIPS FOR BETTER SPELLING

Sometimes all we need to correct an error we make regularly is to use a mnemonic (memory aid) device. If spelling is not your strong suit, you might find the following information helpful.

How many times have you checked a word in a dictionary, only to refer to a dictionary again for the same word because you couldn't remember the correct spelling? Following are four tips to help you correctly spell some of your problem words.

SPELLING—MNEMONICS

1. Basic Method

- Use a dictionary
- Look at the word in syllables
- Say it aloud in syllables
- Visualize and say aloud
- Write it out fully

This method involves the use of five senses to aid your memory, (seeing, saying, hearing, visualizing, writing).

2. Shortcut Method

- Locate the trouble spot in a word (the place where you misspell it)
- Isolate the sound
- Underline the trouble spot
- Emphasize it by mispronouncing it with the correct letter sound:

    SEP-A-RATE; FA-TI-GUE

- Look for short words in the long word:

    ARGUMENT (GUM)

    ENVIRONMENT (IRON)

    CEMETERY (MET)

SPELLING—MNEMONICS (continued)

3. Gimmicks

- What sound would you emit in a <u>cemetery</u>? "Eee!"
  (there are three e's in cemetery)

- The accident oc<u>cur</u>red on the <u>RR</u> tracks (double the r's)

- L<u>oo</u>se as a g<u>oo</u>se (rhyming)

4. Helpful to Know

- The "i" before "e" except after "c" and when sounded like "a" as in "neighbor" and "weigh" rule applies to 1,000 words in the English language

- Doubling the final consonant rule governs 3,000 words

- The reason "offered" does not double the "r" and "referred" does is because the accent is on the first syllable, so the last consonant is not doubled before adding the ending.

Accent on First Syllable	Accent on Second Syllable
layering	occurring
offered	referred
programed	preferred
canceled	remitted
benefited	omitted

- Most plurals are formed simply by adding "s"

- Apostrophe "s" ('s) should never be used to form plurals except to avoid confusion (e.g., CPAs, not CPA's; but "dot your <u>i's</u>")

- British spelling sometimes differs from American spelling. For example,

British	American
judgement	judgment
colour	color
draught	draft
defence	defense
centre	center

IMPROVE YOUR PUNCTUATION!

People are often either good spellers or they aren't. Punctuation errors, on the other hand, can trouble everyone. Fortunately, of the 30 main punctuation marks, business people require fewer than a dozen for writing. Of these, the comma (,), colon (:), semicolon (;), and apostrophe (') are most often used—incorrectly! These are the four punctuation marks we have chosen to cover. Please carefully read the next few pages. We have included only the highlights of punctuation pointers, but we hope we've included solutions to some of the problems that trouble you.

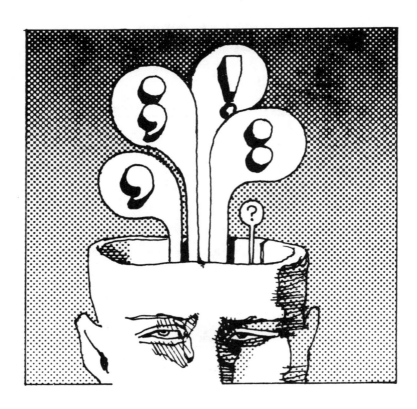

PUNCTUATION POINTERS

THE COMMA (,)

The comma sets off or separates words or groups of words within sentences.

---

1. Use a comma after a long introductory phrase or clause: ''After working all day at the office, I went home for dinner.''

2. If the introductory material is short, forget the comma: ''After work I went home for dinner.''

3. But use it if the sentence would be confusing without it, like this: *NOT*, ''The day before I borrowed my boss's calculator.''
   BUT, ''The day before, I borrowed my boss's calculator.

4. Use a comma to separate elements in a series: ''I enjoy drinking orange juice, tea, milk, and coffee.''

5. Use a comma to separate independent clauses that are joined by:
   and, but, or, nor, for, yet ''We shopped for three hours, *but* we didn't make a single purchase.''

6. Use a comma(s) to set off *nonessential* elements in a sentence. Compare these two sentences:

   ''At the podium stood a man wearing a green suit.'' [''wearing a green suit'' is essential to identify which man]

   ''At the podium stood Frank, wearing a green suit.'' [''wearing a green suit'' adds nonessential information about Frank.)

Recognize and correct comma faults (i.e., two sentences separated only by a comma).

NOT, He bought his first car last winter, it never ran well.

BUT, He bought his first car last winter. It never ran well.

OR, He bought his first car last winter, but it never ran well.

OR, He bought his first car last winter; it never ran well.

The comma fault can be corrected by any one of the three ways listed above.

If you use however, moreover, therefore, consequently, nevertheless, or then between two independent clauses (i.e., sentences by themselves), you must use one of the following: 1. period, 2. semicolon, or 3. comma plus conjunction between the two clauses.

NOT, It looked difficult, therefore, we did not try.

BUT, It looked difficult. Therefore, we did not try.

OR, It looked difficult; therefore, we did not try.

OR, It looked difficult, and therefore we did not try.

PUNCTUATION POINTERS (continued)

SEMICOLON (;)

The semicolon separates two independent clauses, but it keeps those two thoughts more tightly linked than a period can: "I type letters; he types bills."

Use a semicolon *before* and a comma *after* the following words if the words come between two independent clauses:

accordingly	hence	moreover	similarly
also	however	namely	still
besides	likewise	nevertheless	then
consequently	indeed	nonetheless	therefore
furthermore	instead	otherwise	thus

"I thought I had completed the project; consequently, I was surprised to hear about the additional work."

"We have prepared your estimate; however, you should sign it by Friday."

"The partner's retreat will be held in March; therefore, all business matters will be discussed then."

COLON (:)

A colon is a tip-off to get ready for what's next: a list, a long quotation, or an explanation. It's used to separate independent clauses when the second clause explains or amplifies the first.

"Fred was proud of his sister: she had been promoted to managing partner."

"My new office contains the following items: a partner's desk, a leather chair, and oak paneling."

"We need additional information: escrow statements, tax returns, approved bank loans, and mortgage agreements."

"It is safe to predict what overhead costs will do next year: they will go up."

"There are two things to remember in a job interview: always arrive promptly and always dress appropriately."

APOSTROPHE (')

An apostrophe is commonly used to form the possessive of nouns and some pronouns and to mark the omission of letter(s) in a contraction.

If the noun is singular, add 's:
"I enjoyed Betty's presentation." "Someone's coat is in the lobby."

The same applies for the singular nouns ending in 's' like James;
"This is James's new office."

If the noun is plural, simply add an apostrophe after the s:
"Those are the clients' files."

If the singular noun ends in s, add es' to make it both plural and possessive:
"Here is the Dickenses' tax information."

PUNCTUATION EXERCISE

DIRECTIONS: Punctuate the following; then compare your answers with those on page 61. Not all of the sentences need additional punctuation.

1. The executive watched the competition but the competition went ahead with the takeover.

2. During our meeting she was genial but shrewd.

3. Today more women are becoming executives in corporations.

4. The job was difficult therefore he quit.

5. My suitcase included files pencils books and paper.

6. We thought we would have to work late consequently we were happy to be home before dark.

7. My boss car was in the shop however she borrowed her husbands.

8. In preparation for the meeting Mr. Jones asked us to do three things set up the equipment dust the chairs and empty the ashtrays.

9. We wanted to go to the partners meeting but we were unable to leave before the weekend.

10. Lois résumé arrived yesterday moreover she phoned for an interview next week.

PARALLEL CONSTRUCTION

Parallel construction adds clarity, elegance, and symmetry to your writing. Words, phrases and statements are coordinated to be grammatically parallel: noun aligned with noun, verb with verb, and phrase with phrase. For example,

1. NOT: Speaking in public is sometimes harder than to write in private.

   BUT: Speaking in public is sometimes harder than writing in private.

2. NOT: My partner is a man of action, decision, and who is bright.

   BUT: My partner is a man of action, decision, and intelligence.

3. NOT: Sarah's office was painted, had carpeting put in and paneled last week.

   BUT: Sarah's office was painted, carpeted, and paneled last week.

4. NOT: To teach, to supervise, and delegating work are a few of the tasks our office manager performs.

   BUT: To teach, to supervise, and to delegate work are a few of the tasks our office manager performs.

   OR: Teaching, supervising, and delegating work are a few of the tasks our office manager performs.

Not only does parallel construction add symmetry, it often reduces wordiness—see examples #2 and #3 above. Don't hesitate, however, to repeat a word if it makes your sentence clearer. For example,

1. NOT: She has and continues to seem competent.

   BUT: She has seemed and continues to seem competent.

2. NOT: A secretary can program a computer to type a letter but not think

   BUT: A secretary can program a computer to type a letter but not to think.

When you proofread your work, check for parallel construction. The added clarity and economy will add polish to your style.

PARALLEL CONSTRUCTION EXERCISE

Revise the following sentences to form correct parallel construction. Write your answers in the space provided following each sentence. Then, turn to page 62 to compare your responses with the author's.

1. It was both a long meeting and very tedious.

2. Mark enjoys his work as a contractor during the day and going to the ballgame in the evening.

3. Business used to be taught by the textbook method, while today the practical-experience method is used.

4. Choices competing for an executive's free time and that require little energy have decreased dramatically.

5. Poor writing costs money, wastes time, and customers feel alienated.

PROPER WORD USAGE

Proper word usage is another problem for business people. Entire books are written on this subject. The quiz below will test your knowledge of proper usage. If you wish to sharpen your skills, there are two books you should add to your library: *The Elements of Style, 3rd Edition* by Strunk and White (MacMillan Publishing Co. Inc., New York, NY) and *On Writing Well* (Third Edition) by William Zinsser (Harper & Row, Publishers, New York). Both books are interesting, easy to read, and discuss proper word usage.

A USAGE QUIZ

INSTRUCTIONS: Read each item below and circle or fill in the correct answer(s). After you complete the exercise, turn to page 62 and compare your answers with those of the author.

1. Which is correct?

   a. affect/effect
   b. effect/effect
   c. effect/affect
   d. affect/affect

The _____ of wearing seatbelts can _____ the number of people injured in automobile accidents.

2. Which is correct?

   a. The party pledges not to raise taxes, which would be harmful to the economy.
   b. The party pledges not to raise taxes that would be harmful to the economy.

3. Which is correct in business writing? (Circle the correct one in each pair.)

   a. 6 *or* six
   b. 14 *or* fourteen
   c. 500 years ago . . . *or* Five-hundred years ago . . .
   d. 4.5 million *or* 4,500,000

4. Which is correct?

   a. Was 22 July 19XX the date of ball game?
   b. On July 22, 19XX I graduated from business school.
   c. On July 22, 19XX, I'm leaving on vacation.

5. Which is correct?

   a. An historic choice.
   b. A historic choice.

A USAGE QUIZ (continued)

6. Which is correct?

    a. He implied that we were not to blame.
    b. He inferred that we were not to blame.

7. Which is correct?

The boss can _____ all the files _____ the ones we receive today.

    a. except/except
    b. accept/except
    c. accept/accept
    d. except/accept

8. Which is correct?

I would _____ you to follow the _____ of your supervisor.

    a. advice/advise
    b. advise/advice
    c. advise/advise
    d. advice/advice

9. Which is correct?

We were _____ to leave when Mrs. Smith asked us if we had _____ been given a copy of the agenda.

    a. all ready/already
    b. already/already
    c. all ready/all ready
    d. already/all ready

10. Complete each sentence using either *capitol* or *capital*.

    a. Austin is the _____ of Texas.
    b. The company tried to raise enough _____ to buy new equipment.
    c. Paris is the _____ of France.
    d. The first word in a sentence should begin with a _____ letter.
    e. If you want to watch state government in action, visit the _____ in Sacramento, California.

PART 2 STYLE

The word ''style'' means how language is used. The beginning of this section discusses the problem of wordiness in writing—a common problem. Too often people clutter their message with unnecessary words and redundant expressions. Wordiness usually means authors don't have a clear idea of what they want to say, and they don't choose their words carefully. It also means they don't take time to edit what they have written.

On the facing page is an exercise to help you recognize and eliminate wordiness in writing.

WORDINESS EXERCISE I

How can you clarify or simplify to improve the terms and expressions on this list? This exercise will help you identify and eliminate wordiness, jargon, and "purple prose."

terminate the illumination	lights out
revenue commitment	tax increase
at this point in time	_____
in the event of	_____
due to the fact that	_____
at a later date	_____
jumped off of	_____
on a daily basis	_____
each and every one	_____
firstly	_____
in my opinion, I think	_____
irregardless	_____
owing to the fact that	_____
there is no doubt but that	_____
so very happy	_____
clenched tightly	_____
close proximity	_____
close scrutiny	_____
in the majority of instances	_____
at this juncture of maturation	_____
in an intelligent manner	_____

Compare your answers with those of the author on page 64.

REDUNDANT EXPRESSIONS

Sometimes people use too many words because of redundant expressions. Look closely at the list on the facing page. Many of these expressions sound right because we hear them so often, but notice how many words we can eliminate with no loss in meaning.

Add your own examples of redundant expressions to this list.

(UNNECESSARY) REDUNDANCIES

The following list contains common redundant expressions. Delete the word or words in parentheses.

(advance) planning

ask (a question)

(as to) whether

(as) yet

(at a) later (date)

at (the) present (time)

(basic) fundamentals

(specific) example

(but) nevertheless

(close) proximity

(close) scrutiny

combine (together)

(completely) filled

consensus (of opinion)

continue (on)

estimated at (about)

(exact) opposites

first (of all)

for (a period of) 10 days

(just) exactly

my (personal) opinion

(absolutely) essential

(as) for example

refer (back)

(true) facts

(when and) if

whether (or not)

written (down)

(brief) moment

off (of)

period (of time)

might (possibly)

since (the time when)

recur (again)

(still) remains

(thorough) investigation

sufficient (enough)

started (off) with

merged (together)

repeat (again)

blend (together)

came (at a time) when

(false) pretenses

(on a) daily (basis)

_____

_____

_____

_____

WORDINESS EXERCISE II

Now that you've learned to recognize and eliminate wordiness, this exercise provides additional practice pruning what you write. You may rewrite each, but make sure that the original meaning is not lost. After you've completed the exercise, turn to page 65 and compare your answers with those of the author.

1. It has been my wish for a considerable period of time to gain entrance into the field of accounting. This is due to the fact that challenges of my intellect are what challenge me.

2. To me it appears that Smith did not give attention whatsoever to the suggestion that had been recommended by the consultant.

3. In the past there were a quite large number of firms located on the West Coast offering us competiton. At this present point in time, the majority of those firms have been forced to go out of business by the hardships and difficulties of the present recessionary period of business contraction and stagnation.

4. It is the policy of this company in every case to proceed with care in testing each and every new product under development by us, and such testing must precede our arriving at any positive conclusion with respect to the effectiveness of said product.

5. In the event that Wilkins does not come forth with an expression of willingness to lend us assistance in the matter of financing this project, it is entirely conceivable that we will not be able to make the required acquisitions of raw materials we need without help.

PITFALLS OF BUSINESS WRITING

Following is a list of twelve common problems in business writing, followed by more detailed descriptions of each pitfall. You are invited to make this list more personal by jotting down other examples you've encountered.

PITFALLS OF BUSINESS WRITING	page
1. **Too Many Words**	24
2. **Clichés**	24
3. **Too Many Big Words**	24
4. **Jargon**	25
5. **Vague Expressions**	25
6. **Condescending Statements**	25
7. **Sexist Language**	25
8. **Negative Expressions**	26
9. **Inattention to Detail**	26
10. **Inattention to the Reader**	26
11. **Lack of Commitment**	26
12. **Passive Construction**	27

(Add your own)

_____

_____

_____

_____

PITFALLS OF BUSINESS WRITING

1. **Too Many Words**
   - One word is better than two.
   - A good rule is to limit your sentences to fewer than 17 words.
   - Edit ruthlessly.

   > *NOT:* In this letter we have attempted to answer all of your questions, and we hope that if you have any additional questions whatsoever, please do not hesitate to contact us.
   >
   > *BUT:* If you have additional questions, please call us.

2. **Clichés**
   - Avoid fad words and trite phrases like "input," "parameters," "utilize," "hopefully," and "enclosed please find."

   > *NOT:* Enclosed please find the information per your request. Hopefully, you can utilize our product to benefit your company within the parameters of your computer's invoice processing. We appreciate your input.
   >
   > *BUT:* We have enclosed the information you requested. Our product will speed your computer's invoice processing. Thank you for your suggestions.

3. **Too Many Big Words**
   - Keep your writing simple: use "home" instead of "abode," "face" instead of "visage," "use" instead of "utilize."
   - Short words are better than long words.
   - Try to be natural in your writing.
   - Read your letters aloud after you write them; they should sound human and conversational.

   > *NOT:* Pursuant to our discussion, herewith we acknowledge receipt of your correspondence as of the above date.
   >
   > *BUT:* We received your letter on December 16 as we discussed.

PITFALLS OF BUSINESS WRITING (continued)

4. Jargon
- Avoid unexplained terms like "facilitator" and "interface."
- What is a "modified departmentalized schedule"?

> *NOT:* Our facilitator will interface with the new communication systems network.
>
> *BUT:* Our administrative assistant will operate the new telephone system.

5. Vague Expressions
- Be concise and specific.
- If the "profits were affected" did they increase or decrease?

> *NOT:* The company's negative cash flow position forced it to resize its operations to the level of profitable market opportunities.
>
> *BUT:* The company lost money and had to lay off workers.

6. Condescending Statements
- Write with warmth, as one human to another.
- "Of course" can be interpreted "as any idiot knows."

> *NOT:* We are certain you are concerned with saving money. Of course you will mail the enclosed card. We thank you in advance.
>
> *BUT:* If saving money is important to you, please mail the enclosed card today. Thank you.

7. Sexist Language (See page 45 for more information on this.)
- Consider your reader. (The salutation "Gentlemen" is outdated.)
- **Traditionally, "he," "his," and "him" were neutral pronouns, yet there are alternatives you can use to avoid offending your reader.**
- Use "he or she" sparingly.
- Here are other suggestions:

> *NOT:* An accountant must pass a difficult exam before he can become a CPA.
>
> *BUT (use plurals):* Accountants must pass a difficult exam before they can become CPAs.
>
> *OR (avoid using pronouns whenever possible):* **An accountant must pass a difficult exam before becoming a CPA.**
>
> *OR:* To become a CPA, an accountant must pass a difficult exam.
>
> *OR (use "you" when appropriate—if you know your audience!):* As an accountant, you must pass a difficult exam before you become a CPA.

PITFALLS OF BUSINESS WRITING (continued)

8. Negative Expressions

- Stress the positive.
- Instead of telling what you can't do or don't have, provide good news.

> *NOT:* We're sorry to tell you that we don't carry XYZ software.
>
> *BUT:* Since we no longer carry XYZ software, we are sending you a list of distributors who do carry the software.

9. Inattention to Detail

- Triple check accuracy and quality.
- Reread for typos and misspelled words.

> *NOT:* We hope we can accomodate your office supply and stationary needs.
>
> *BUT:* We hope we can accommodate your office supply and stationery needs.

10. Inattention to the Reader

- Write in the first person when appropriate.
- Write in the second person when possible.
- Remember to write from the reader's perspective.

> *NOT:* We would like to invite you to attend the conference.
>
> *BUT:* You are invited to attend the conference

11. Lack of Commitment

- Take a stand.
- Omit qualifiers—''sort of,'' ''rather,'' ''quite,'' ''somewhat.''

> *NOT:* We are quite pleased about our rather exciting word processor.
>
> *BUT:* We are pleased about our exciting line of word processors.

PITFALLS OF BUSINESS WRITING (continued)

12. **Passive Construction**
   - Use active verbs.
   - The normal order of sentences is subject (performer of action), verb, and object (receiver of action). In passive contruction, the order is reversed: the object is first, followed by a form of the verb "be" (am, is, are, was, were, been, being) before the main verb; then, the subject is last (usually preceded by the word "by"). For example,

---

PASSIVE: The check <u>was signed</u> by my boss.[7 words]

The letter <u>is being typed</u> by the secretary. [8 words]

He practices what <u>has been learned</u>. ["By him" is implied.]

ACTIVE: My boss <u>signed</u> the check. [5 words]

The secretary <u>is typing</u> the letter. [6 words]

He practices what <u>he has learned</u>.

   - Sometimes writers use passive construction and leave out the subject of the sentence. For example,

---

PASSIVE: An employee's extra efforts <u>should be recognized</u>. [By whom?]

ACTIVE: Bosses should <u>recognize</u> an employee's extra efforts.

PASSIVE: Enclosed are your schedules.

ACTIVE: I enclose your schedules.

   - Active construction is almost always more direct, more economical, and more foreceful than passive construction.
   - As you proofread your work, be sure you have:
     1. Stated the subject (performer of the action) of each sentence.
     2. Placed the subject of each sentence before the object (the receiver of the action).
     3. Used the verb "be" cautiously—overuse weakens your writing.

FIVE STYLISTIC TOOLS

Can you see the importance of style in business writing? The facing page lists five stylistic tools to help polish your writing. You may find it helpful to photocopy and refer to this page to refresh your memory about important techniques to use in order to write well.

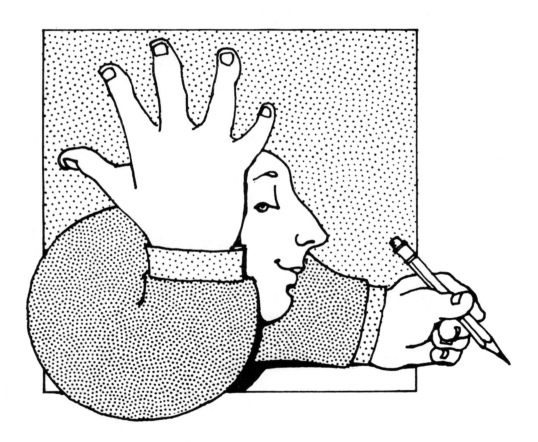

FIVE STYLISTIC TOOLS

1. **LEARN TO RECOGNIZE AND AVOID TRITE EXPRESSIONS AND CLICHÉS. EXAMPLES INCLUDE:**

   - along these lines
   - as per our agreement
   - at the present time
   - due to the fact that
   - enclosed please find
   - for the purpose of
   - in response to your memo of
   - in view of the fact
   - per
   - pursuant to
   - regarding the matter of
   - we are returning same herewith
   - as per your request
   - at an early date
   - despite the fact that
   - enclosed herewith
   - for the amount of
   - in response to your letter of
   - pending receipt of
   - please be advised
   - thank your for your cooperation
   - we will file your letter for future reference
   - with reference to your letter of
   - subsequent to

2. **TRIM UNNECESSARY WORDS.** If a word does not serve a purpose, omit it. Watch for redundant expressions. For example,

   ''Please ~~be advised that~~ complete these adjustments ~~must be completely finished~~ within ~~a period of~~ three weeks. Thank you ~~for your interest in and attention to this matter.~~''

3. **USE ACTIVE (VS. PASSIVE) CONSTRUCTION:**

Passive:	It was necessary to terminate the search.	(seven words)
Active:	I decided to stop looking.	(five words)
Passive:	The secretary was hired by Mary.	(six words)
Active:	Mary hired the secretary.	(four words)

4. **BE SPECIFIC:**

   Vague: The woman sat there reading a magazine.
   Specific: Mabel sat on the couch reading *McCalls*.

   Vague: The recall affected their profits. [How did it affect them? Increase? Decrease?]

5. **USE SIMPLE WORDS:**

   Complex: Subsequently, we'll require your endorsement.
   Simple: Later we'll need your signature.

PART 3 BUSINESS WRITING

This section contains actual writing samples of letters and memos. All samples contain weaknesses and errors common in business writing. Some of the weaknesses are more subtle than others. Please read each sample carefully, and evaluate each stage: the ''before'' version, the ''corrected'' version, and the ''improved'' version.

WRITING SAMPLES

DESCRIPTION: John Freeman, President of ABC Enterprises, requested his accountant to explain why his accounting bill doubled since last year. Following is the accountant's response.

BEFORE

XYZ ACCOUNTING CORPORATION
1420 Fremont Way
Oakdale, CA 95123
(805) 772-4322

July 2, 19XX

Mr. John Freeman
ABC Enterprises

Dear John:

In response to your letter of June 15, 19XX, enclosed please find Exhibit A. As you can see, the work performed for you this year is different than last year. In addition, the parameters of tasks increased since last year. Accordingly due to this fact and the fact that our billing rates were raised this year; it was necessary to increase our charges for professional services rendered. Hopefully, this letter offers some explanation as to the question you raised. If you require more additional information, please don't hesitate to contact us.

Sincerely,

XYZ Accounting Corporation

WRITING SAMPLES (continued)

CORRECTED

XYZ ACCOUNTING CORPORATION
1420 Fremont Way
Oakdale, CA 95123
(805) 772-4322

July 2, 19XX

Mr. John Freeman
ABC Enterprises
2027 Washington Blvd.
Oakdale, CA 95123

Dear John:

[TRITE] In response to your letter *[USE "FROM"]* of June 15, 19XX, *[CLICHE']* enclosed please find
Exhibit A. *[CONDESCENDING]* As you can see, the work performed for you this year *[JARGON]*
is different *[than]* last year. In addition, the *[parameters]* of tasks *[OMIT]*
increased since last year. *[OMIT]* Accordingly due to this fact and the fact *[PASSIVE]*
that our billing rates were raised this year; it was necessary to *[OMIT]*
increase our charges for professional services rendered. *[USE "ANSWERS"]* Hopefully,
this letter offers some explanation as to the question you raised.
If you require more additional information, *[REDUNDANT]* please don't hesitate *[WORDY]*
[WORDY] to contact us.

Sincerely,

XYZ Accounting Corporation

WRITING SAMPLES (continued)

IMPROVED

XYZ ACCOUNTING CORPORATION
142O Fremont Way
Oakdale, CA 95123
(8O5) 772-4322

June 25, 19XX

Mr. John Freeman
ABC Enterprises
1000 Welch Way
Fountain Canyon, AZ 84666

Dear John:

We understand your concern, and we hope the following will
answer your questions regarding the increase in our bill:

1. Last year we spent 12 hours (@ $80/hour) preparing two tax
   returns for you.

2. This year we spent 15 hours (@ $100/hour) preparing four
   tax returns for you.

3. This year we successfully represented you in an audit with the
   Internal Revenue Service (3 hours @ $100/hour).

4. This year we produced monthly financial statements for you,
   whereas last year we produced quarterly financial statements.

Please call me if you would like to discuss this further. We value
you as a client.

Sincerely,

XYZ Accounting Corporation

by Marianne Evers, CPA

ME/jdc

WRITING SAMPLES (continued)

EMPLOYMENT AGENCY COUNSELOR'S LETTER

Following is a letter from an employment agency counselor to businesses announcing a new telephone communication setup.

BEFORE

```
September 5, 19XX


Dear Employer:

We have established a special phone communication system to provide
additional opportunities for your input.  During this year we will give
added emphasis to the goal of communication and utilize a variety of
means to accomplish this goal.  Your input, from the unique position
of employer, will help us to plan and implement an effective plan that
meets the staffing needs of your company.  An open dialogue, feedback
and sharing of information between employment counselors and employers
will enable us to work with your staffing needs in the most effective
manner.


Sincerely,

Ted F. Jones
Employment Counselor
```

WRITING SAMPLES (continued)

CORRECTED

September 5, 19XX

Dear Employer:

We have established a special phone communication system to provide
additional opportunities for your input. During this year we will give
added emphasis to the goal of communication and utilize a variety of
means to accomplish this goal. Your input, from the unique position
of employer, will help us to plan and implement an effective plan that
meets the staffing needs of your company. An open dialogue, feedback
and sharing of information between employment counselors and employers
will enable us to work with your staffing needs in the most effective
manner.
Sincerely,

Ted F. Jones
Employment Counselor

(Annotations: JARGON, VAGUE, USE "USE", UNCLEAR, STILTED)

IMPROVED

September 5, 19XX

Dear Employer:

We have established a special phone system to improve the
communication between employment counselors and employers.
Please call our office any afternoon between 4:00-5:00 if you
have questions about available applicants or if you'd just
like to talk. We believe that if we encourage you to call,
we can establish a closer relationship and better meet your
staffing needs.

Sincerely,

Ted F. Jones
Employment Counselor

[This revised version of the letter sounds much more human.]

WRITING SAMPLES (continued)

MEMO

A sales manager asked his administrative assistant to send a memo (along with a copy of quarterly sales figures) to the sales staff asking them to meet with him on the following Friday. The result follows.

POORLY WRITTEN

MEMORANDUM

TO: All Sales Representatives
FROM: Jim Martin
DATE: July 15, 19XX
SUBJ: Sales Meeting

Re phone contact of July 8, final sales totals for the quarter ended June are enclosed herewith. A planning conference for all sales personnel will be scheduled for the near future and these figures will be discussed. It is hoped that all district managers will be aware that the figures are such that reductions in the total number of dealerships and retail units may be indicated. A meeting to discuss this matter will be held on Friday, 18 July, at 3 p.m., in the regional manager's office. Thank you for your cooperation.

IMPROVED

MEMORANDUM

TO: All Sales Representatives
FROM: Jim Martin
DATE: July 15, 19XX
SUBJ: Sales Meeting

Please attend a sales meeting on Friday. July 18 at 3 p.m. in the regional manager's office. We will discuss the attached quarterly sales totals.

This meeting is important because we may have to reduce dealerships and retail units.

[Note how direct and clear the revised version is. The sentences are brief and to the point. Also, the revised version is more natural and conversational without sounding too informal.]

NINE TIPS FOR A BETTER MEMO

1. Get to the point quickly—the reader already knows the purpose of the memo because of the subject line.

2. Be interesting, conversational, natural.

3. Highlight key ideas (*, -, or •); make it readable.

4. Keep it short—use 17 or fewer words per sentence generally.

5. Write in A-B-C order (sequentially).

6. Be specific, clear, concise, and economical.

7. Keep your reader(s) in mind.

8. Keep it simple.

9. Keep it to one page.

CONVEYING BAD NEWS TACTFULLY

Often in business we must break bad news to good people. This is one time where brevity and conciseness take a back seat to tact and humanity. In other words, your tone is all important. Choose your words carefully; select words that are human, courteous, and positive. Don't use qualifiers, passive construction, and euphemisms to avoid accepting responsibility. For example, a company president wrote the following to her employees:

> *"It is necessary to resize our operation to the level of profitable market opportunities."*

What she meant was this:

> *"We must lay off staff."*

Note the difference between the following positive and negative phrases:

NEGATIVE	POSITIVE
You failed to notice	*May I point out that*
You neglected to mention	*We also can consider*
You overlooked the fact	*One additional fact is*
You missed the point	*From another perspective*
If you persist in	*If you choose to*
I see no alternative but	*Our clear plan of action*

Generally, a memo to correct an employee's behavior is more effective if sentences begin with a word other than "you." Whenever possible, avoid overusing YOU.

HOW TO SAY NO:

At times we must clearly deny an employee's request. Be direct and considerate, but don't be too subtle; otherwise, you may mislead by offering false hope instead of communicating clearly. Often "no" means "no": it's the packaging that's all important. Remember: even criticism can be delivered positively.

SAMPLE BAD NEWS MEMOS

One of your employees has been eagerly awaiting a transfer to the company's San Francisco office. Write a memo to tell him the transfer will not take place.

BEFORE

MEMORANDUM

TO: John Williams
FROM: Marsha Brown
DATE: May 12, 19XX
RE: Denial of your request for transfer

I regret to inform you that your request for transfer to our San Francisco office has been denied. At this point in time, there are no positions open for which you are qualified. Thank you for your understanding.

BAD NEWS MEMOS (continued)

IMPROVED

MEMORANDUM

```
TO:      John Williams
FROM:    Marsha Brown
DATE:    May 12, 19XX
RE:      Response to transfer request

After we spoke last week, I checked into the possibility of your
transferring to our San Francisco office.  Unfortunately, I
learned a transfer is not currently possible for two reasons.
First, our department needs your experience and skills for new
product marketing.  Second, this year San Francisco is expanding
its accounting department only.

I am sorry your proposed transfer did not work out.  Please let
me know if I can assist you in any other way.
```

Note the difference in packaging. Both memos clearly deny the request, but the ''before'' version sounds mechanical, stuffy, and cold. Although you want to be clear and concise in your writing, don't sacrifice kindness. ''Concise'' and ''brief'' don't have the same meaning. When you must give bad news to good people, take the time to select words that are tactful and kind.

BASIC OUTLINE FOR BUSINESS LETTERS

The outline on the facing page will help you to structure your business letters. Almost all business letters have three main parts: an introduction, a body, and a conclusion. This outline offers other considerations to help transform adequate writing into quality writing. It reviews the techniques of providing a preview of your main points in the introduction, and a transition statement between each section.

Transitions are often neglected in writing. They serve as stepping stones between the main ideas to help the letter flow more smoothly. Transitions can be as short as one or two words—e.g., ''furthermore'' or ''in addition''—or a transition can be an entire sentence—e.g., ''Now that we've examined the possibilities, let's select the route that's best for you.''

Not every letter you write will have three main ideas previewed in the introduction and developed in the body, but this outline can help organize your thoughts, so the reader will be able to clearly understand what you are communicating.

BASIC OUTLINE FOR A BUSINESS LETTER

INTRODUCTION

I.   Opening statement(s). This is your attention step

II.   Topic sentence.   This states reason for writing.

Previews   { A. Single sentence.   states 1st major idea
the   { B. Single sentence.   states 2nd major idea
Content   { C. Single sentence.   states 3rd major idea

[Transition statement—one sentence to get you from the introduction to the body]

BODY

III.   First major idea of the letter, expressed in a single sentence.
    A. Explain your first idea
    B. Support your first idea
    C. Conclude your first idea

[Transition statement]

IV.   Second major idea of the letter developed like the one above.

[Transition]

V.   Third major idea of the letter developed like the first one.

[Transition]

CONCLUSION

VI.   Summary of the major ideas (if the letter is lengthy or complex)

VII.   Closing statement(s)

BASIC OUTLINE FOR BUSINESS
LETTERS (continued)

Although all business letters don't need to be outlined first, you'll find it helpful to draft all letters before they are typed. Whether you outline or use a rough draft, you should organize your ideas in ABC order. The basic outline for business letters on the preceding page will help you organize your message.

On the facing page is a sample letter using the outline. Following the sample is the sample letter in final form.

SAMPLE OUTLINED LETTER

INTRODUCTION

I. Do you understand all the changes that will take place with the new tax laws? Although the laws will benefit many people, there are changes you need to be aware of to protect your investments.

II. Following are three ways you can take advantage of changes to the new legislation.

Preview
of the
Content

    A. Purchase any automobiles or major appliances before the end of the year.

    B. Open an IRA (Individual Retirement Account) and contribute $2,000 before next April 15.

    C. Call our office to set up an appointment with one of our professional tax advisors.

[Transition statement—I will explain these steps in detail.]

BODY

III. Purchase any automobiles or major appliances before the end of the year.
    A. You can deduct the sales tax on your tax return.
    B. Because of the new tax laws, this will be the last year that sales tax is deductible.
    C. So if you planned to make these purchases, do not wait until the new year.

[Transition statement—Our next suggestion could also save you money.]

IV. Open an IRA.
    A. You can contribute $2,000 by next April 15 and still deduct the entire amount for the current year.
    B. The new laws reduce the amount you can deduct beginning next year.
    C. So you should consider taking advantage of this tax-savings opportunity now.

[Transition—Although these steps help you save money in two ways, an appointment with us could help you even more.]

V. Call our office.
    A. We can provide specific information to meet your individual needs.
    B. We will review your current financial position.
    C. And provide additional ways to benefit from changes in the laws.

[Transition—If you are concerned about the tax law revisions and how they affect you, consider the recommendations we discussed.]

CONCLUSION

VI. The new tax laws are confusing. You can, however, benefit from the changes if you know what steps to take now. Please call our office today for more information.

SAMPLE LETTER FROM OUTLINE

November 1, 19XX

Dr. Sarah Alexander
123 Middlebury Avenue
Cromwell, CA 94092

Dear Dr. Alexander:

19XX Tax Law Revision Update

Do you understand the changes in the new tax laws? Although the laws
will benefit many people, there are changes you need to be aware of to
protect your investments.

Following are three ways you can protect yourself from financial worries
next year:

* Purchase any automobiles or major appliances before the end
  of the year.
* Open an IRA (Individual Retirement Account) and contribute
  $2,000 before next April 15.
* Call our offices for an appointment with one of our tax
  advisors for personal service.

To appreciate the prospective benefits of these steps, I have explained
them below.

If you purchase automobiles or major appliances before the end of the
year, you can deduct the sales tax on your tax return. This will be
the last year that sales tax is deductible. If you plan to make these
purchases, act before the end of the year.

In addition, you may also contribute $2,000 to an IRA by April 15 and
still deduct the entire amount. The new laws place restrictions on IRAs
beginning next year, so you should consider taking advantage of this tax-
saving opportunity now.

Although the above steps can help you save money, an appointment with
us could help even more. We can provide specific information to meet
your individual needs. We will review your present financial position
and suggest additional ways you can benefit from changes in the laws.

If you are concerned about the effect of the new tax laws, please call
our office today for more information.

Sincerely,

SMITH, STEWART, AND STONEY
A PROFESSIONAL ACCOUNTING CORPORATION

JSS/slb

AVOIDING SEXISM IN BUSINESS WRITING

The increasing numbers of women in business has changed many traditional practices. One change is the updating of business correspondence to include women. For decades the salutation in most letters was ''Gentlemen.'' This is no longer suitable, and alternatives must be considered. Following are some acceptable forms of address.

INSTEAD OF: **USE:**

      Gentlemen: Dear Partners:

                                Dear Doctors:

                                Dear Directors:

                                Dear Educators:

                                Dear Shareholders:

                                Dear Members:

                                add your own _____

In other words, use a more specific—and nonsexist—title of your reader in the salutation.

Many companies omit the salutation and complimentary close. Letters are simplified to emphasize their message and streamline their form. The following letter demonstrates this idea.

March 26, 19XX

Personnel Manager
Sanders Enterprises, Inc.
1425 Seaview Way
Daily City, CA 93456

                    SPECIAL PHONE SYSTEM*

We have established a special phone system to improve the communication between employment counselors and employers. Please call our office any afternoon between 4:00–5:00 if you have questions about available applicants or if you would just like to talk. We believe that if we encourage employers to call, we can establish a closer relationship with you and better meet your staffing needs.

Ted F. Jones
Employment Counselor

---

*The subject line may be placed flush left to conform with the block style of the letter or be centered as it is here.

EXERCISE: WRITING A BUSINESS LETTER

You should now be prepared to write a complete letter using the information you've learned. Refer to the preceding sections as you organize your thoughts, and remember to avoid the common pitfalls of business writing. After you write your letter, turn to page 66 and compare it with the author's example. Although your letter will be different from the model in the Appendix, it will be well written if you avoided unnecessary words, jargon, or vague words, and you organize it using the basic outline shown on page 41.

INSTRUCTIONS: Write a letter to Mark Smith who has applied for a position with your firm. Keep the following points in mind: your letter will be rejecting him, he has good qualifications, and you would like more information about him should another position open.

(You should outline and/or draft your letter on a separate sheet)

NOTE: This page may be used to copy the final version of your letter.

PART 4 | WRITING PERSUASIVELY

Congratulations on your progress thus far! You have completed the foundations of learning to write well. Now that you've practiced the basics, we're going to progress to the next level, which is learning to write persuasively.

Some people avoid using the word *persuasion* because it conjures images of manipulation and deceit. This is unfortunate because most communication is persuasive. Anytime you influence or affect people you're being persuasive. Isn't it true that everything you write in business affects the reader, whether it's a memo, invoice, or client proposal letter?

This section provides information on communicating persuasively and offers you an opportunity to write a persuasive letter using the skills you have acquired in this book.

Here is a good first rule: SHOW HOW YOUR READER WILL BENEFIT. In other words, don't tell your clients how great your photocopier is, but tell them how great their copies will look.

Aristotle said, "The fool tells me his reasons, but the wiseman persuades me with my own."

PERSUASION—BITS AND PIECES

I. Persuasion is human communication designed to influence an audience.

- Credibility is essential to create audience behavior or attitude changes

- Credibility factors

    1. Do you appear trustworthy?
    2. Do you have expertise?
    3. Are you dynamic?
    4. Will your reader identify with your message?

- Persuasion often doesn't occur in a single event—it takes time

II. Persuasion in Business

- Useful in these areas:

    1. Proposals to prospective clients
    2. Salary negotiations with your boss
    3. Feasibility reports
    4. Recommendations
    5. Employment interviews
    6. Sales—advertising and promotion

    Add your own _____

- Tailor your writing to your reader's:

    1. Background
    2. Experience
    3. Knowledge
    4. Interests
    5. Responsibilities
    6. Perceptions
    7. Needs
    8. Values

MOTIVATED SEQUENCE

The Motivated Sequence Outline (described on the facing page) is effective when you prepare a persuasive letter, report, or speech. Read through each step, then turn the page and review the sample essay that follows the Motiviated Sequence Outline.

You should test the effectiveness of your persuasive letters by applying the five steps of the Motivated Sequence Outline. If your letter gets the attention of the readers, shows the readers how an existing problem affects them, solves the problem, explains what your solution will do, and encourages readers to adopt your solution, then you have written an effective persuasive letter.

MOTIVATED SEQUENCE OUTLINE

Specific Purpose: On a separate sheet of paper write a complete sentence stating exactly what you hope to accomplish in your letter. This gives you focus. As you write your letter, remember your specific purpose to keep your message on track.

I. **Attention Step**

    A. Overcome readers' apathy

    B. Helpful to use illustration, example, etc.

II. **Need Step**

    A. Show why change is needed

    B. Show why readers need to feel affected by the problem

III. **Satisfaction (of need) Step**

    A. State solution

    B. Demonstrate that solution is logical, makes sense and is feasible

    C. Convince that solution will solve problem

    D. Give examples where solution has worked

IV. **Visualization (of future) Step**

    A. Show readers what solution will do for them

    B. State advantages

V. **Action Step**

    A. Convince readers to adopt solution

    B. Tell readers specifically what you want them to do

    C. Direct readers to act

MOTIVATED SEQUENCE OUTLINE MODEL

Learning to Communicate Effectively is Crucial to Your Career

I. Attention Step

    A. Anecdote—"A middle-aged, factory worker enrolled in a class to help him learn to read. The teacher began by showing him words he was used to seeing around the factory. They had just begun when he recoiled. 'Is _that_ what that word means?' he asked. For years the man had been sneaking cigarettes under a sign. And he never knew the sign read DYNAMITE."

    B. This story doesn't apply to you. Or, does it?

[Transition: Let's find out.]

II. Need Step

    A. A 1982 survey conducted by the Association of American Colleges showed that 92% of the corporations cited communication skills as the most sought after quality in job applicants.

    B. _Changing Times_ February 1985 stated that the best advice for graduating seniors is the development of written and oral communication skills to the highest possible degree.

    C. How certain are you that school has taught you to communicate effectively?

        1. Have you learned communicating to impress and not to express?

        2. Are you guilty of: vagueness, poor construction, jargon, wordiness, or clichés?

    D. You're being given an opportunity to become an effective communicator; can you really afford to turn it down?

    E. The fact is, you must learn how to communicate effectively to enjoy a successful career.

[Transition: What can you do to learn this?]

III. Satisfaction Step

    A. The solution I'm offering is clear and easy to understand.

MOTIVATED SEQUENCE OUTLINE MODEL
(continued)

    B. The steps include these techniques:

        1. Keep your writing clear and concise.

        2. Choose your words carefully.

        3. Be natural.

    C. The solution is a challenge to practice.

        1. Don't become frustrated and give up.

        2. Old habits die hard.

[Transition: Perhaps you're asking yourself, ''How will I know the solution will work?'']

IV. Visualization Step

    A. Listen to the difference in the following statements:

        1. A speechwriter for Franklin Roosevelt wrote: ''We are endeavoring to construct a more inclusive society.''

        2. Franklin Roosevelt changed it to this: ''We're going to make a country in which no one is left out.''

        3. The difference is in using familiar words.

[Transition: What am I asking you to do?]

V. Action Step

    A. All you need is to read and apply the lessons as presented in <u>BETTER BUSINESS WRITING.</u>

        1. Ten steps to effective communication are clearly stated.

        2. Read them carefully.

        3. Practice them every time you write.

        4. Don't get discouraged; writing is hard work.

    B. The quality of the final product will be your reward.

    C. Learn and practice this solution, and unlike the middle-aged factory worker, you'll never have to play with dynamite.

YOUR FINAL EXERCISE

This final exercise allows you to use everything you've learned in this book, including the fundamentals of writing persuasively. Refer to pages 48-53 as a review before you begin to write. After you finish your letter, turn to page 67 and compare it with the example in the Appendix. Your letter will be different from the sample, yet it can be effective if you have followed the advice presented in this book. The sample offers an alternative approach to writing persuasively.

WRITING PERSUASIVELY

INSTRUCTIONS: In the space below, write a proposal letter to a prospective client (Dr. Steven James) outlining the services your firm can offer. Remember that you are attempting to convince Dr. James to select your firm.

REVIEW

For a general review, the facing page offers a summary of the most important points discussed in this book. You might find it helpful to refer to this page often, particularly the "Ten Techniques for Effective Communication." Make it a habit to read through the list whenever you practice writing to incorporate these techniques.

At first, you may find that old habits die hard, and that when you attempt to improve your writing, it will take you longer to write even routine letters. You may be tempted to pull from the "community soup of words and phrases" (jargon and clichés) to pad your letters. You may become frustrated as your stare at a blank pad or as your wastebasket fills with crumpled paper. Don't despair! Writing is hard work, but the quality of the final product is the key to greater rewards. Good luck!

NOTE: An excellent companion book to BETTER BUSINESS WRITING is now available. To receive a copy of WRITING FITNESS use the order form on page 71 of this book.

THE TEN COMMANDMENTS FOR MORE EFFECTIVE COMMUNICATION

1. Keep your writing clear, concise and simple.

2. Choose your words carefully.

3. Be natural.

4. Avoid fad words, jargon, and clichés.

5. Use active verbs; avoid passive construction.

6. Take a stand, make a commitment, avoid qualifiers.

7. Use familiar words—plain English.

8. Be specific: avoid vagueness.

9. Eliminate redundant expressions.

10. Keep your audience in mind.

58

OTHER SUGGESTIONS TO SHARPEN YOUR WRITING SKILLS: AVOID JARGON, JOURNALESE, QUALIFIERS AND INTENSIFIERS

JARGON—"shoptalk"; special words found in the workplace. There are two problems with jargon: it often sounds pretentious, and its meaning is often obscure.

JOURNALESE—"pre-fab" words patched together out of other parts of speech. Journalese is usually faddish and short-lived. Search for existing words to state what you want.

JARGON	JOURNALESE	
parameters	"Greats"	
interface	"Notables"	adjectives as nouns
input	"Peer group"	
utilize	"Top officials"	
optimize	"Health reasons"	nouns as adjectives
maximize	"Insightful"	
prioritize	"To host"	
quantify	"Impact"	nouns as verbs
potentialize	"Enthuse"	nouns chopped off to form verbs
paradigm		

Scientific jargon: The biota exhibited a 100% mortality response.

Translation: All the fish died.

QUALIFIERS—dilute your meaning. For example,

QUALIFIERS: so, rather, quite, pretty much, kind of, sort of, like (as in "He's, you know, like smart"), a bit.

NOT: "She's a rather effective administrator."

BUT: "She's an effective administrator."

The second sentence expresses commitment, whereas the first sentence avoids taking a stand. Good professional writing is lean and confident.

INTENSIFIERS—can be appropriate in casual conversations. Professional writing seldom needs the extreme tone of intensifiers.

INTENSIFIERS: great, literally, really, definitely, certainly, totally, absolutely

APPENDIX: SOLUTIONS AND AUTHOR RESPONSE TO EXERCISES.

SOLUTION TO SPELLING EXERCISE—PAGE 7

1. The applicant studied Freudian __PSYCHOLOGY__ (-chology) in college.

2. Ms. Brown wanted us to sit __TOGETHER__ (tog-th-r) at the meeting so we would not be __SEPARATED__ (sep-r-ted) when the meeting was over.

3. The new hotel can __ACCOMMODATE__ (acco-date) up to 1,500 guests.

4. This memo __SUPERSEDES__ (super-edes) the __PRECEDING__ (prec-ding) one which was distributed last week.

5. The Hospital __BENEFIT__ (Ben-fit) raised a lot of money for the children's wing.

6. It never __OCCURRED__ (oc-ur-ed) to us that the __GOVERNMENT__ (gove-ment) might increase our taxes.

7. The secretary's boss __OFFERED__ (of-er-ed) her a bonus if she would __PROCEED__ (proc-d) to enroll in a shorthand class.

8. We successfully avoided an __ARGUMENT__ (arg-ment) when we discussed changing the __ENVIRONMENT__ (envi-ment) of the office to boost employee morale.

9. The hinges on the door are __LOOSE__ (l-se) and it __CONSISTENTLY__ (consist-ntly) rattles when opened.

10. It would be difficult not to __BELIEVE__ (bel-ve) the results.

61

SUGGESTED SOLUTION
PUNCTUATION EXERCISE —PAGE 13

1. The executive watched the competition, but the competition went ahead with the takeover.

2. During our meeting she was genial but shrewd.

>   No punctuation needed. The introductory phrase is short and doesn't require a comma. Note there is no comma before the phrase ''but shrewd'' because it is not an independent clause.

3. Today more women are becoming executives in corporations.

>   No punctuation needed.

4. The job was difficult; therefore, he quit.

   OR: The job was difficult. Therefore, he quit.

   OR: The job was difficult, and therefore he quit.

5. My suitcase included files, pencils, books, and paper.

>   NOTE: There is no colon after ''included'' because a colon must follow a complete sentence such as:

>   ''My suitcase included four items: files, pencils, books, and paper.''

6. We thought we would have to work late; consequently, we were happy to be home before dark.

   OR: We thought we would have to work late. Consequently, we were happy to be home before dark.

7. My boss's car was in the shop; however, she borrowed her husband's.

8. In preparation for the meeting, Mr. Jones asked us to do three things: set up the equipment, dust the chairs, and empty the ashtrays.

9. We wanted to go to the partners' meeting, but we were unable to leave before the weekend.

10. Lois's résumé arrived yesterday; moreover, she phoned for an interview next week.

Better Business Writing

SUGGESTED SOLUTIONS (continued)

PARALLEL CONSTRUCTION EXERCISE —PAGE 15

1. The meeting was both long and tedious.

2. Mark enjoys working as a contractor during the day and going to the ballgame in the evening.

3. Business used to be taught by the textbook method; today it is taught by the practical-experience method.

4. Choices competing for an executive's free time and requiring little energy have decreased dramatically.

5. Poor writing costs money, wastes time, and alienates customers.

A USAGE QUIZ —PAGE 16

1. Which is correct?

   The ___EFFECT___ of wearing seatbelts can ___AFFECT___ the number of people injured in automobile accidents.
   a. affect/effect
   b. effect/effect
   X c. effect/affect
   d. affect/affect

   Affect is usually a verb while effect can be both a noun and a verb. Affect generally mean: ''to influence.'' Effect can mean both ''result,'' and ''to bring about a change.''

2. Which is correct?

   a. The party pledges not to raise taxes, which would be harmful to the economy.
   b. The party pledges not to raise taxes that would be harmful to the economy.

   Both sentences are correct depending on your meaning. The first sentence refers to all taxes. It's saying, in effect, that all taxes are harmful to the economy. (b) is referring to special taxes, but the party may raise other taxes that would not be harmful to the economy. In (a), ''which'' introduces a nonrestrictive clause, meaning it's simply adding some nonessential information about taxes; that's why it's set off by commas. In (b), ''that'' introduces a restrictive clause, meaning it's providing essential information about the taxes just mentioned.

SUGGESTED SOLUTIONS (continued)

A USAGE QUIZ (continued) —PAGE 16

3. Which is correct in business writing?

   a. 6 *or* six
   b. 14 *or* fourteen
   c. 500 years ago . . . *or* Five-hundred years ago . . .
   d. 4.5 million *or* 4,500,000

   > In formal writing, numbers one to ten are written as words, 11 and over as numerals; always write out numbers if they begin a sentence; both 4.5 million and 4,500,000 are correct.

4. Which is correct?

   X a. Was 22 July 19XX the date of the ball game?
     b. On July 22, 19XX I graduated from business school.
   X c. On July 22, 19XX, I'm leaving on vacation.

   > Dates within sentences are correct written either like (a.) or (c.) Dates written as in (a.) do not require a comma following the year. Dates written in the conventional style (c.) need a comma following the year.

5. Which is correct?

     a. An historic choice.
   X b. A historic choice.

   > b. is correct.

6. Which is correct?

   a. He implied that we were not to blame.
   b. He inferred that we were not to blame.

   > Both are correct depending on your meaning. Implied means to suggest, infer means to assume or conclude.

7. Which is correct?

   The boss can ____ACCEPT____ all the files ____EXCEPT____ the ones we receive today.

     a. except/except
   X b. accept/except
     c. accept/accept
     d. except/accept

   > Accept means to take what is offered.
   > Except means to leave out; to omit.

A USAGE QUIZ (continued)

8. Which is correct?

   I would ___ADVISE___ you to follow the ___ADVICE___ of your supervisor.

   a. advice/advise
   X b. advise/advice
   c. advise/advise
   d. advice/advice

   > Advice is a noun meaning a suggestion about how to do something or
   > what to do.
   > Advise is a verb meaning to give advice.

9. Which is correct?

   We were _ALL READY_ to leave when Mrs. Smith asked us if we had
   ALREADY been given a copy of the agenda.

   X a. all ready/already
   b. already/already
   c. all ready/all ready
   d. already/all ready

   > All ready is an adjective meaning everyone or everything is prepared.
   > Already is an adverb meaning previously.

10. Complete each sentence using either *capitol* or *capital*.

    a. Austin is the ___CAPITAL___ of Texas.
    b. The company tried to raise enough ___CAPITAL___ to buy new equipment.
    c. Paris is the ___CAPITAL___ of France.
    d. The first word in a sentence should begin with a ___CAPITAL___ letter
    e. If you want to watch state government in action, visit the ___CAPITOL___ in
       Sacramento, California.

Use capitol only when you are referring to the building. Mnemonic device—
remember that most capitOl buildings have a dOme.

WORDINESS EXERCISE I —PAGE 19

terminate the illumination	lights out
revenue commitment	tax increase
at this point in time	now
in the event of	when

WORDINESS EXERCISE I (continued)—PAGE 19

due to the fact that	due to or because
at a later date	later
jumped off of	jumped off
on a daily basis	daily
each and every one	all
firstly	first
in my opinion, I think	use one or the other
irregardless	regardless
owing to the fact that	due to
there is no doubt but that	undoubtedly
so very happy	happy
clenched tightly	clenched
close proximity	close
close scrutiny	scrutinize
in the majority of instances	usually
at this juncture of maturation	now
in an intelligent manner	intelligently

WORDINESS EXERCISE II —PAGE 22

1. I have always wanted to go into accounting because it challenges me.

2. I believe Smith ignored the consultant's suggestion.

3. Many of our West Coast competitors have gone out of business because of the recession.

4. It is company policy to carefully test all new products for effectiveness.

5. If Wilkins does not help us financially, we may not be able to acquire needed raw materials.

SUGGESTED SOLUTION (continued)

WRITING A BUSINESS LETTER EXERCISE —PAGE 47

August 14, 19XX

Mr. Mark Smith
100 Elm Street
Glenville, WA 98888

Dear Mark:

Thank you for applying to XYZ Corporation for the position of staff accountant. Although we presently do not have any openings, we expect to interview again in December. Your resume is impressive, and we will keep it on file if a staff accountant position should become available before December.

Meanwhile, please send us three letters of recommendation to complete your application package. We appreciate your interest.

Sincerely,

XYZ CORPORATION

by William R. Houghton

SUGGESTED SOLUTION (continued)

WRITING PERSUASIVELY EXERCISE —PAGE 55

September 21, 19XX

Dr. Steven James
6495 Meridian Way
Franklin Way
Franklin, CA 93868

Dear Dr. James:

Thank you for requesting information about our firm. I will introduce you to our company and discuss some of the valuable services we provide.

XYZ Company has grown from 150 clients to our current 1,500. Our policy is to take on only as many clients as we can attend to personally. Many of our original clients are still with us.

Twenty-five percent of our current clients are doctors. Because of our experience with physicians, we have developed expertise in determining which services will most benefit those in the medical profession. We provide the following special services:

1. Analyzing your financial position to determine if your
    practice will benefit by incorporation.

2. Preparing your tax returns.

3. Automating your bookkeeping and monthly accounting
    records on our in-house computer system.

After 26 years in this business, we are proud of the quality of our clients and the services we provide. We are certain we will provide the best service for you, too.

Please call us if you have questions. We look forward to hearing from, and working with you.

Sincerely,

Bill Armstrong
XYZ ACCOUNTING CORPORATION

ENTER A LEARNING CONTRACT

A definition of ACCOUNTABILITY is to be responsible for one's actions.

We all have good intentions. The thing that separates those who are successful from those who are not is how well these ''good intentions'' are carried out.

A Voluntary Contract (or Agreement) can help convert your good intentions into action.

The Voluntary Learning Contract on the facing page is a good starting point if you are serious about getting the most from this book.

This Agreement can be initiated by either you, or your supervisor, either as you begin working in this book, or after you have completed it.

CONSIDER A VOLUNTARY CONTRACT

VOLUNTARY
LEARNING CONTRACT*

I, _____, agree
   (Your name)

to meet with the individual designated below at the times shown
to discuss my writing skills progress. The purpose of all sessions
will be to *review* my writing skills and establish action steps in areas
where improvement may still be required.

I agree to meet with the above individual on:

_____

_____

_____

_____

(described schedule giving date and times)

_____

Signature of supervisor or instructor.

Areas needing attention:
- ☐ Spelling
- ☐ Punctuation
- ☐ Usage
- ☐ Style
- ☐ Writing Persuasively
- ☐ Other _____

_____

My Signature   *Date*

NOTES

NOTES

NOTES

Quantity	Title	Code #	Price	Amount
	MANAGEMENT TRAINING			
	Self-Managing Teams	00-0	$7.95	
	Delegating for Results	008-6	$7.95	
	Successful Negotiation — Revised	09-2	$7.95	
	Increasing Employee Productivity	10-8	$7.95	
	Personal Performance Contracts — Revised	12-2	$7.95	
	Team Building — Revised	16-5	$7.95	
	Effective Meeting Skills	33-5	$7.95	
	An Honest Day's Work: Motivating Employees	39-4	$7.95	
	Managing Disagreement Constructively	41-6	$7.95	
	Learning To Lead	43-4	$7.95	
	The Fifty-Minute Supervisor — 2/e	58-0	$7.95	
	Leadership Skills for Women	62-9	$7.95	
	Coaching & Counseling	68-8	$7.95	
	Ethics in Business	69-6	$7.95	
	Understanding Organizational Change	71-8	$7.95	
	Project Management	75-0	$7.95	
	Risk Taking	076-9	$7.95	
	Managing Organizational Change	80-7	$7.95	
	Working Together in a Multi-Cultural Organization	85-8	$7.95	
	Selecting And Working With Consultants	87-4	$7.95	
	Empowerment	096-5	$7.95	
	Managing for Commitment	099-X	$7.95	
	Rate Your Skills as a Manager	101-5	$7.95	
	PERSONNEL/HUMAN RESOURCES			
	Your First Thirty Days: A Professional Image in a New Job	003-5	$7.95	
	Office Management: A Guide to Productivity	005-1	$7.95	
	Men and Women: Partners at Work	009-4	$7.95	
	Effective Performance Appraisals — Revised	11-4	$7.95	
	Quality Interviewing — Revised	13-0	$7.95	
	Personal Counseling	14-9	$7.95	
	Giving and Receiving Criticism	023-X	$7.95	
	Attacking Absenteeism	042-6	$7.95	
	New Employee Orientation	46-7	$7.95	
	Professional Excellence for Secretaries	52-1	$7.95	
	Guide to Affirmative Action	54-8	$7.95	
	Writing a Human Resources Manual	70-X	$7.95	
	Downsizing Without Disaster	081-7	$7.95	
	Winning at Human Relations	86-6	$7.95	
	High Performance Hiring	088-4	$7.95	
	COMMUNICATIONS			
	Technical Writing in the Corporate World	004-3	$7.95	
	Effective Presentation Skills	24-6	$7.95	
	Better Business Writing — Revised	25-4	$7.95	

Quantity	Title	Code #	Price	Amount
	COMMUNICATIONS (continued)			
	The Business of Listening	34-3	$7.95	
	Writing Fitness	35-1	$7.95	
	The Art of Communicating	45-9	$7.95	
	Technical Presentation Skills	55-6	$7.95	
	Making Humor Work	61-0	$7.95	
	50 One Minute Tips to Better Communication	071-X	$7.95	
	Speed-Reading in Business	78-5	$7.95	
	Influencing Others	84-X	$7.95	
	PERSONAL IMPROVEMENT			
	Attitude: Your Most Priceless Possession — Revised	011-6	$7.95	
	Personal Time Management	22-X	$7.95	
	Successful Self-Management	26-2	$7.95	
	Business Etiquette And Professionalism	32-9	$7.95	
	Balancing Home & Career — Revised	35-3	$7.95	
	Developing Positive Assertiveness	38-6	$7.95	
	The Telephone and Time Management	53-X	$7.95	
	Memory Skills in Business	56-4	$7.95	
	Developing Self-Esteem	66-1	$7.95	
	Managing Personal Change	74-2	$7.95	
	Finding Your Purpose	072-8	$7.95	
	Concentration!	073-6	$7.95	
	Plan Your Work/Work Your Plan!	078-7	$7.95	
	Stop Procrastinating: Get To Work!	88-2	$7.95	
	12 Steps to Self-Improvement	102-3	$7.95	
	CREATIVITY			
	Systematic Problem Solving & Decision Making	63-7	$7.95	
	Creativity in Business	67-X	$7.95	
	Intuitive Decision Making	098-1	$7.95	
	TRAINING			
	Training Managers to Train	43-2	$7.95	
	Visual Aids in Business	77-7	$7.95	
	Developing Instructional Design	076-0	$7.95	
	Training Methods That Work	082-5	$7.95	
	WELLNESS			
	Mental Fitness: A Guide to Emotional Health	15-7	$7.95	
	Wellness in the Workplace	020-5	$7.95	
	Personal Wellness	21-3	$7.95	
	Preventing Job Burnout	23-8	$7.95	
	Job Performance and Chemical Dependency	27-0	$7.95	
	Overcoming Anxiety	29-9	$7.95	
	Productivity at the Workstation	41-8	$7.95	
	Healthy Strategies for Working Women	079-5	$7.95	
	CUSTOMER SERVICE/SALES TRAINING			
	Sales Training Basics — Revised	02-5	$7.95	
	Restaurant Server's Guide — Revised	08-4	$7.95	
	Effective Sales Management	31-0	$7.95	

Quantity	Title	Code #	Price	Amount
	CUSTOMER SERVICE/SALES TRAINING (continued)			
	Professional Selling	42-4	$7.95	
	Telemarketing Basics	60-2	$7.95	
	Telephone Courtesy & Customer Service — Revised	64-7	$7.95	
	Calming Upset Customers	65-3	$7.95	
	Quality at Work	72-6	$7.95	
	Managing Quality Customer Service	83-1	$7.95	
	Customer Satisfaction — Revised	84-1	$7.95	
	Quality Customer Service — Revised	95-5	$7.95	
	SMALL BUSINESS/FINANCIAL PLANNING			
	Consulting for Success	006-X	$7.95	
	Understanding Financial Statements	22-1	$7.95	
	Marketing Your Consulting or Professional Services	40-8	$7.95	
	Starting Your New Business	44-0	$7.95	
	Direct Mail Magic	075-2	$7.95	
	Credits & Collections	080-9	$7.95	
	Publicity Power	82-3	$7.95	
	Writing & Implementing Your Marketing Plan	083-3	$7.95	
	Personal Financial Fitness — Revised	89-0	$7.95	
	Financial Planning With Employee Benefits	90-4	$7.95	
	ADULT LITERACY/BASIC LEARNING			
	Returning to Learning: Getting Your G.E.D.	02-7	$7.95	
	Study Skills Strategies — Revised	05-X	$7.95	
	The College Experience	07-8	$7.95	
	Basic Business Math	24-8	$7.95	
	Becoming an Effective Tutor	28-0	$7.95	
	Reading Improvement	086-8	$7.95	
	Introduction to Microcomputers	087-6	$7.95	
	Clear Writing	094-9	$7.95	
	Building Blocks of Business Writing	095-7	$7.95	
	Language, Customs & Protocol	097-3	$7.95	
	CAREER BUILDING			
	Career Discovery	07-6	$7.95	
	Effective Networking	30-2	$7.95	
	Preparing for Your Interview	33-7	$7.95	
	Plan B: Protecting Your Career	48-3	$7.95	
	I Got The Job!	59-9	$7.95	
	Job Search That Works	105-8	$7.95	

	Amount
Total Books	
Less Discount	
Total	
California Tax (California residents add 7%)	
Shipping	
TOTAL	

☐ Please send me a free Video Catalog.   ☐ Please add my name to your mailing list.

 ☐ Mastercard   **VISA** ☐ VISA   **AMERICAN EXPRESS** ☐ AMEX   Exp. Date _____

Account No. _____   Name (as appears on card) _____

Ship to: _____   Bill to: _____

_____   _____

_____   _____

_____   _____

Phone number: _____   P.O. #: _____

**All orders of less than $25.00 must be prepaid. Bill to orders require a company P.O.#.
For more information, call (415) 949-4888 or FAX (415) 949-1610.**